Calisthenics for Beginners

A Beginner's Guide to Bodyweight Training

© Copyright 2016 - All rights reserved.

This document is geared towards providing exact and reliable information in regards to the topic and issue covered. The publication is sold with the idea that the publisher is not required to render accounting, officially permitted, or otherwise, qualified services. If advice is necessary, legal or professional, a practiced individual in the profession should be ordered.

- From a Declaration of Principles which was accepted and approved equally by a Committee of the American Bar Association and a Committee of Publishers and Associations.

In no way is it legal to reproduce, duplicate, or transmit any part of this document in either electronic means or in printed format. Recording of this publication is strictly prohibited and any storage of this document is not allowed unless with written permission from the publisher. All rights reserved.

The information provided herein is stated to be truthful and consistent, in that any liability, in terms of inattention or otherwise, by any use or abuse of any policies, processes, or directions contained within is the solitary and utter responsibility of the recipient reader. Under no circumstances will any legal responsibility or blame be held against the publisher for any reparation, damages, or monetary loss due to the information herein, either directly or indirectly.

Respective authors own all copyrights not held by the publisher.

The information herein is offered for informational purposes solely, and is universal as so. The presentation of the information is without contract or any type of guarantee assurance.

The trademarks that are used are without any consent, and the publication of the trademark is without permission or backing by the trademark owner. All trademarks and brands within this book are for clarifying purposes only and are the owned by the owners themselves, not affiliated with this document.

Wait! Before you continue....
Would you like to like to have access to **FREE KINDLE BOOKS?**

If you answered **YES** then CLICK HERE

http://bit.ly/1t755d8

There is a FREE BONUS at the end of the book!

Go to the end of the book to get the 10% discount and to give me your Image.

table of contents

Introduction 1

Chapter 1 What is Calisthenic Training? 2
   Basic Requirements for Calisthenics 3

Chapter 2 Importance of Warm up and Flexibility in Calisthenics .. 5
   Importance of Warm-up 6
   Importance of Body Flexibility 7

Chapter 3 Benefits of Calisthenics 8

Chapter 4 10
   Upper Body Exercises 13
   Core Calisthenics Exercises 40
   Lower Body Calisthenics 64
   Full Body Calisthenics 72

Chapter 5 Supplementation for Overall Health and Fitness 106

Finish 112

Introduction

I want to thank you and congratulate you for downloading the book, *"Calisthenics for Beginners"*.

Stick to the instructions in this book and get the well-toned, firm body you have always desired. The extremely useful workouts in this guide will help in achieving your fitness goals.

Thanks again for downloading this book. I hope you enjoy it!

Chapter 1
What is Calisthenic Training?

An array of body weight light exercises performed to achieve general fitness and psychomotor skills. Nowadays, calisthenics are generally performed as a street workout to build well-defined and stronger muscles through several different body weight exercises.

Through calisthenics exercises, you can improve your agility, coordination, aerobic capacity and balance more than an Olympic athlete. In calisthenics, you can push, pull, bend or swing your body in different directions by using your body weight for resistance to make these movements more intense and efficient.

Basic Requirements for Calisthenics

Calisthenics is not as easy it looks like; it includes a variety of body weight exercises that cannot be performed without an adequate muscular strength, core stability and strength.

Here are some basic needs for calisthenics;
- A proper warm-up for better joint activation
- More than adequate body flexibility and strength
- Agility, balance, and coordination
- Core stability and strength

In sports and games, your body's strength and flexibility play a key role in improving your moves and your fitness level. If you have bulky, strong body muscles without the strong and stable core, then you cannot perform several callisthenic moves that an intermediate practitioner of calisthenics can perform with ease. Calisthenics requires great body strength along with the stable and strong core.

Chapter 2
Importance of Warm up and Flexibility in Calisthenics

Importance of Warm-up

Warm-up not only prepares our body muscles and mind for different physical activities but also improves the range of motion of muscles involved. A proper warm-up minimizes sports injuries, improves blood flow, increases body temperature, promotes energy generation system within our body and enhances physical performance. It has medically proven that an appropriate warm-up improves the production of necessary hormones that stimulate our body to generate sufficient energy.

8 to 10 minutes warm-up is an adequate warm-up that prepares your body for intense exercises and difficult postures with ease by activating our joints and muscles involved.

Do a proper warm-up and add some stretching exercises to make it more effective, because warming up your body means to expand blood vessels that reduce stress on the heart by reducing the resistance.

Importance of Body Flexibility

Flexibility exercises not only keep our joints active but also improve the range of motion of our body muscles involved in these exercises. Flexibility exercises allow us to perform different difficult moves with ease and comfort by improving our body's performance. For truly perfect calisthenics, flexibility plays a vital role. In the way of perfection and progression, flexibility is the path and the strength is the ability to walk on to reach your destination (perfect Calisthenic moves). Dynamic and static stretching exercises after your warm-up and workouts keep you flexible and strong as well.

Chapter 3
Benefits of Calisthenics

All types of body weight training keep our muscles and joints active and powerful. There is no doubt that body weight training has been an essential part of bodybuilding and other sports. Nowadays, Calisthenic workouts are being like by the majority of the fitness lovers or conscious. Here are some benefits of bodyweight training;

- Being a physiological activity, body weight training improves our cardiovascular health, strengthens bones, promote muscle health and boost body metabolism as well
- Since body weight exercises or calisthenics target multiple body muscles, therefore these exercises burn extra calories and help our body in losing unnecessary weight
- All body weight exercises shape our body and help in developing beautiful & strong muscles for life
- One of the most salient benefits is that calisthenics do not need any equipment like in weight training
- There are several calisthenics that can be practiced at home or anywhere you find some spare time
- Being a natural exercise, calisthenics improve bone and muscle mass dramatically
- A moderate practitioner of calisthenics have more strong and stable core than a weight training practitioner
- Through appropriate calisthenics, you can build great strength and stamina without losing flexibility. Several Calisthenic exercises consist of dynamic and static stretching exercises that improve the range of motion of muscles involved
- I have discovered a strange truth about calisthenics and that is "calisthenics develop creativity in you while performing different Calisthenic exercises"

Chapter 4
Calisthenics Exercises

In this chapter following exercises are mentioned:

1. Wide handed Pushups *
2. Standard pushups *
3. Incline pushups *
4. Triangle or diamond pushups *
5. Standard Pull-ups *
6. Chest high pull-ups *
7. Clap pull-ups *

8. Typewriter pull-ups *
9. "L" sit pull-ups *
10. Chin-ups *
11. Burpees *
12. Lunges *
13. Walking lunges *
14. Crunches *
15. Crisscross crunches *
16. Side toe touching *
17. Side-to-side *
18. Sit-ups *
19. Standard Plank hold *
20. Side plank hold *
21. Back leg raise plank hold *
22. Jumping jack or stride jumps *
23. Inverted "L" hold Toe touches *
24. Squats *
25. Explosive squats *
26. One leg squat or bullet squat *
27. Incline leg hold *
28. Crocodile raise *
29. "L" hold *
30. "V" hold *
31. "L" sit raise *

32. Full length side raise *

33. Knee rotation on high bar *

34. Windshield wipers

35. Bar dips *

36. Calf raise *

37. High bar swing *

38. Wall handstand *

39. Modified handstand pushups *

40. Wall handstand pushups *

41. Muscle ups on bar *

42. Bridge hold *

43. Bridge pushups *

44. "L" hold bar dips *

45. Frog jumping *

46. Bench crocodile raise *

47. Side leg raise *

48. Front leg raise *

49. Back leg raise *

50. Dragon flag *

Upper Body Exercises

Incline Pushups

Instructions:

Incline pushups provide you more support to perform this exercise with ease and comfort. Incline pushups are easy to perform when you rest your hands on a high place while resting your feet on a lower ground and are more challenging when you rest your hands on a lower ground while resting your feet on a higher ground to make an incline.

Standard pushups

Pushups is an effective body weight training that you can perform in a variety of ways to target different body muscles. Standard pushups primarily target your chest and arm muscles and secondarily targets core muscles.

Instructions:

* Start by holding standard plank position by supporting your whole body weight on your toes and your arms (straight)
* Lower your upper body to touch the ground and then move back to starting position
* Repeat this exercises 10 to 15 times to complete one set

Wide Handed Pushups

Variations in pushups not only targets different upper body muscle but also makes your workout effective. Wide handed pushups primarily target your chest muscles. Wide handed pushups improve your muscular stability and strength.

Instructions:

* Hold standard plank position with your hands open wider than your shoulder width
* Support your whole body with your hands and toes while keeping your spine straight
* Now, gently move your upper body in downward direction and after reaching near the floor, move back to starting position by straightening your hands
* Repeat 10 to 15 rep if you are a beginner or do as many reps as you can do with ease if you are an advanced practitioner

Diamond Pushups

Diamond pushups is more challenging exercise that primarily targets triceps and requires great muscular stability and endurance.

Instructions:

* Start by holding standard plank position with your arms straight and your hands in a triangle or diamond shape (join thumbs and index fingers of your both hands to make a diamond)
* Now, gently move your upper body down while bending your elbows in sidewise, and then move back to starting position
* Repeat 10 to 15 reps each time
* Do at least 3 sets

Standard Pull-ups

Pull-ups is an advance form of calisthenics or body weight training that requires more than adequate practice. Pull-ups is performed by using a high bar. Pull-ups primarily targets arms, chest, shoulder muscles and latissimus dorsi.

Instructions:

* Grasp a high bar (1-2 feet high above your head) with your both hands little wider than your shoulder width
* Your hand palm should be opposite to your face
* Bend your knees and crisscross your shins
* Now, lift your body up to touch your clavicle bones (bone linking the scapula and sternum) to the bar and then move back to staring position
* Repeat as many reps as you can or according to your fitness level
* Repeat 3 sets

Chest High Pull-ups

Chest high pull-ups are more challenging than standard pull-ups. This exercise exert more stress on your chest, arms and lat muscles.

Instructions:

* Hold the same position of standard pull-ups and touch the end of your chest muscles to the bar
* Do 10-15 reps or according to your fitness level in each set
* Complete 3 sets

Clap Pull-ups

Clap pull-ups is the more challenging exercise than standard and chest high pull-ups.

Instructions:

* Hold standard pull-ups position
* Pull your body up with all your force, quickly clap with your both hands while going up and grasp the bar again before going down
* Avoid jerking and swing while performing clap pull-ups
* Do 8 to 12 reps or as many reps as you can with ease
* Avoid clap pull-ups if you neck strain, back pain, severe muscle soreness and shoulder pain

Typewriter Pull-ups or Archer Pull-ups

Typewriter pull-ups is the more challenging form of pull-ups as compared to standard pull-ups, chest high pull-ups and clap pull-ups.

Instructions:

* Hold pull-ups position while grasping a high bar
* Pull your whole body up and slightly touch your chest to the bar
* Now, firmly hold the bar with your right hand and slide your left-hand parallel to the bar by extending it over the bar
* Do the same for the other hand by holding the bar with your left hand and by sliding your right hand
* Do maximum reps in each set
* Complete three or four sets

"L" Sit Pull-ups

"L" sit pull-ups is an advance technique of pull-ups that is also used in chin-ups. This amazing exercise targets multiple upper body muscles including abdominal core muscles.

Instructions:

* Grasp a high bar with your both hands shoulder width apart like in standard pull-ups
* Raise your both knees in order to make "L" hold and do the same pull-ups
* Do as many reps as you can with ease
* Repeat this exercise in three sets separated by 10 to 20 seconds recovery periods

Muscle up

Muscle up is an advance for of pull-ups.

Instructions:

* Grasp the high bar with your hands little wider than your shoulder width
* Do a standard pull-up and raise your whole body over the bar like in dips by straightening your both arms
* Gently move back to starting position
* Do as many reps as you can
* If you are a beginner, then start this exercise by standing on the ground and jump both feet to reach dips position

Chin-ups

Chin-ups is an amazing exercise that primarily targets biceps and secondarily targets chest muscles.

Instructions:

* Grasp a high bar with your both hands with your hands shoulder width apart or less wide than your shoulder width
* Keep your hand palms towards your face
* Pull your body up to bring your chin closer to bar and then move back to starting position
* Do 10 to 12 reps or according to your fitness level

Burpees

A body weight exercise and is known as sic count body weight training that engages all our body muscles to burn extra calories, to maintain strength and endurance.

Instructions:

* Start by holding squat position by resting your hands by your sides
* Sit on your feet by resting your hands on the ground in front of you
* Jump both feet back to hold pushup position and do a pushup
* Jump your both feet back in towards your hands to hold back squat position again
* Jump from squat position while raising your both hands over your head
* Do 10 to 12 reps or as many reps as you can do with ease

Lunges

Lunges is an effective exercise that primarily targets lower body muscles and secondarily targets abdominal core muscles.

Instructions:

* Stand straight with your one foot apart (from each other)
* Rest your hands on your sides (beginning of pelvis bones)
* Step one foot forward while making 90 degree angle between your thigh and calf, and keep the back leg
* Try to keep your back leg straight (optional or not necessary), but do not move your back foot while forwarding your one foot
* Now move back to starting position and then step forward with your other foot
* Do 15 to 20 reps with each leg
* Repeat three times

Walking Lunges

Walking lunges exert extra stress on the muscles involved in this exercise.

Instructions:

* Stand straight with your feet shoulder width apart
* Step your right foot forward and then hold starting position by pulling your back leg forward, instead of going back
* Repeat by stepping your left foot forward and keep walking in this style for 10 to 20 steps for both legs

Core Calisthenics Exercises

Crunches

Crunches is an impressive exercise that primarily targets abdominal core muscles.

Instructions:

* Lei down on your back with your knees bent and your feet flat on the ground
* Rest your both hands on back of your head without interlacing your fingers to avoid neck pain
* Move your upper body towards your knees without moving your lower body and move back to starting position
* Do 15 to 20 reps or according to your fitness level to complete one set
* Complete 3 sets

Crisscross Crunches

Crisscross crunches is an advanced form of standard crunches.

Instructions:

* Hold standard crunches position with your feet lifted off the ground
* Rest your both hands behind your head
* Touch your right knee to your left elbow while stretching your left leg straight and then move your right knee back
* Now, stretch your right leg straight and touch the left knee to your right elbow
* Continuously repeat this exercise for 30 to 40 seconds to complete one set
* Complete 3 sets

Side Toe Touching

Full-length side toe touching is a core stability and core strengthening exercise that primarily targets internal and external oblique muscles.

Instructions:

* Lie down on your right side (do not lie completely on your back, lie on one of your sides instead)
* Rest your right arm flat on the ground and bend this arm towards your belly to balance your body while performing side toe touching
* Raise your left hand over your head in diagonal direction
* Raise your both legs sidewise and your upper body at the same time to touch your toes with your raised hand (try to make a "V" hold)
* Support your whole body with your hips while making "V" shape
* Now, quickly move back to starting position and repeat this exercise 15 to 20 times
* Do the same exercise for other side

Standard Plank Hold

Standard plank hold strengthens and stables your core muscles.

Instructions:

* Hold pushups positions while supporting your whole body with your toes and your forearms flat on the ground
* Keep your spine straight and your neck while looking horizontally
* Hold this position as long as you can
* Rest for 10 to 15 seconds and start again
* Repeat this exercise for 3 times

Side Plank Hold

Side plank hold primarily targets side abdominal muscles.

Instructions:

* Hold standard plank hold on a padded ground
* Move your body sidewise while lifting your right hand and leg sidewise
* Support your whole body on your left forearm and the left foot
* Hold this position as long as you can with ease
* Do the same exercise for both legs to complete one set
* Complete 2 to 3 sets

Back Leg Raise Plank

Instructions:

* Hold standard plank hold
* gently raise your right leg off the ground (as high as possible with ease and comfort)
* Hold this position as long as you can
* Do this hold for the other leg to complete one set
* Complete two or three sets

Knee Circles

Knee circles is a body weight core strengthening exercise that primarily targets abdominal (front and side belly) muscles.

Instruction:

* Grasp a high bar with your hands shoulder width apart
* Bend your both knees together and make a circle with your knees by rotating them from left to right and vice versa
* Keep your spine straight
* Move your knees in both clockwise and anti-clockwise direction, max reps
* Rest for 20 seconds and then start the next set
* Complete 3 sets

"L" hold

"L" hold is an effective core exercise that targets core muscles and upper body muscles as well.

Instructions:

* Grasp the both bars of a parallel bar while standing between the bars
* Lift your both legs off the ground and keep them straight while making 90 degree angel between your raised legs and belly
* Now, gently raise your whole body from the seat by straightening your hands while keeping your body in "L" shape
* Hold this position as long as you can or according to your fitness level
* Repeat this exercise 3 to 4 times

"V" Hold

Another core strengthening exercise that can be performed without exercising equipment.

Instructions:

* Start by lying on your hips on the ground (padded ground) with your knees bend and feet flat on the ground
* Cross your hands on your chest and stretch straight both your legs in diagonal direction in order to make a "V" shape of your body
* Support your whole body on your hips and keep your spine straight while holding this stance
* Hold as long as you can
* Rest for 10 seconds after each hold
* Repeat this exercise three to four times

Side to Side

A core strengthening exercise that primarily targets oblique muscles.

Instructions:

* Sit on your hips with your knees bent and your feet on the ground
* Make a "V" shape sit like in sit-ups and lift your both feet about 10 to 15 inches off the ground (you can cross your calves) while supporting the whole body on your hips
* Slightly lean back while keeping your spine straight in order to avoid back pain
* Now, interlace the fingers of your both hands and move them towards both right and left sides
* Try to straighten your hands at extreme right and left positions
* Do not move your chest while performing side-to-side
* Complete 3 sets with maximum reps

Full length "L" Sit Raise

A core strengthening exercise that improves abdominal core muscles and exerts a bit stress on hip muscles.

Instructions:

* Hold a high bar with your both hands shoulder width apart
* Straighten your whole body and lift your legs in upward direction in order to touch the bar over your head
* Now, gently move your legs back to starting position without bending them
* Do as many reps as you can to complete one set
* Recover your stamina for 10 to 15 seconds
* Do 3 sets

Full length Side Raise

Full length is another core strengthening exercise performed on a pull-up bar to improve side belly muscles or oblique muscles.

Instructions:

* Hold pull-up position on a pull-up bar
* Keep your whole body straight and gently move both your legs towards right side (diagonally) as high as you can do without feeling any pain (try to touch the bar fixed to the ground or perpendicular to the ground)
* In a gradual manner, move your both legs together back to starting position
* Now, move your legs together towards the left side to complete one rep
* Do 10 to 15 reps in each set
* Complete 3 t 4 sets

Lower Body Calisthenics

Calf Raise

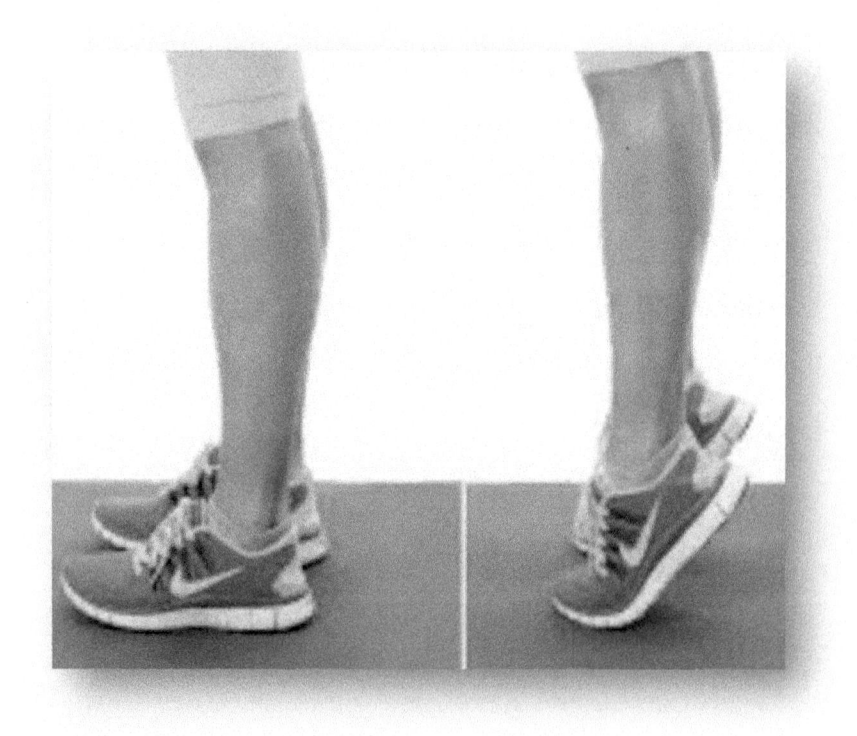

Calf raise is an effective exercise for calf muscles. It is also practiced to improve vertical jump in different sports.

Instructions:

* Stand straight on a box or on the stairs by resting your toes on the edge of a stair step
* Rest your hands on the wall or something else for proper balance
* Gently raise your whole body on your toes as high as you can and then move back to the starting position
* Do as many reps as you can do in a set
* Complete 3 to 4 sets

Squats

Squats is a wonderful body weight exercise to burn extra calories and to improve lower body muscles. This amazing exercise should be added in your routine warm-up or weight loss training.

Instructions:

* Stand straight with your feet a bit wider than should width
* Rest your hands behind your head
* Move your body downward to hold crouching position with your knees bent (try to bend your knees at 90 degree angle between your calves and thighs) while extending your hips in backward direction
* Do not lean your upper body either forward or backward to exactly perform this exercise
* Do maximum reps in each set
* Complete 3 to 4 sets

Explosive Squats

Explosive squats are the advance form of standard squats. This exercise exerts extra stress on your lower body muscles and core muscles as well.

Instructions:

* Hold standard squat position with your hands straight at your sides
* Now, jump from bending position and try to touch your knees to your chest and land in squat position again
* Do as many reps as you can do with ease and stamina in each set
* Complete 3 sets

Bullet Squat or One Leg Squat

A more challenging squat exercise than standard and jump squats.

Instructions:

* Stand straight with your legs shoulder width apart
* Now, move down in sitting position while bending your one leg and straightening your other leg in front of you
* Move back to starting position and repeat this exercise according to your fitness level
* Repeat it three sets

Full Body Calisthenics

Bridge Hold

Bridge hold is an exercise practiced in gymnastics and martial arts to improve upper body flexibility.

Instructions:

* Start by lying on your back on a padded ground with your knees bent and feet flat on the ground
* Rest your hands near ears while facing your fingers of both hands towards your shoulders and your elbows skywards
* Firmly grip the ground with your feet and hands
* Now, lift your upper body off the ground to make a curve or a bridge pose while straightening your elbows
* Try not to move your hands and feet while holding this position
* Hold for 10 to 15 seconds each time
* Rest for 5 to 10 seconds and then do it again
* Repeat this hold three times

Bridge Pushups

Bridge pushups is an advance technique of bridge hold that exerts extra tress on arm muscles.

Instructions:

* Hold bridge position while lifting your body into a bridge position
* Now, move your shoulders downward while bending your elbows (bring your head closer to the ground) without moving your knees
* Do as many pushups as you can in each set
* Complete 3 sets

Wall Handstand

Handstand is an impressing and effective body weight training performed generally in gymnastics. Wall handstand is a beginner handstand training.

Instructions:

* Start by standing near a wall
* Hold handstand position (upside down) with your hands on the ground and your feet resting on a wall to support your handstand
* Try to keep your arms, spine and neck straight while holding this position
* Hold this stance as long as you can

Wall Handstand Pushups

Wall handstand pushups is an advance technique of wall handstand.

Instructions:

* Hold wall handstand position while supporting your body
* Do pushups by bending your elbows and keeping your spine straight
* Support your pushups with your feet resting with the wall
* Do 10 to 15 pushups or as many as you can do with ease

Modified Handstand Pushups

Modified handstand pushups is a good initiative of standard handstand.

Instructions:

* Start by holding wall handstand position with your hands on the ground and your feet with the wall
* Bend your hips while keeping your knees and arms straight while making 90 degree angle between your thighs and belly
* Now, do 10 to 15 pushups in this position
* Rest for 10 to 15 seconds
* Complete 3 to 4 sets

Bar Dips

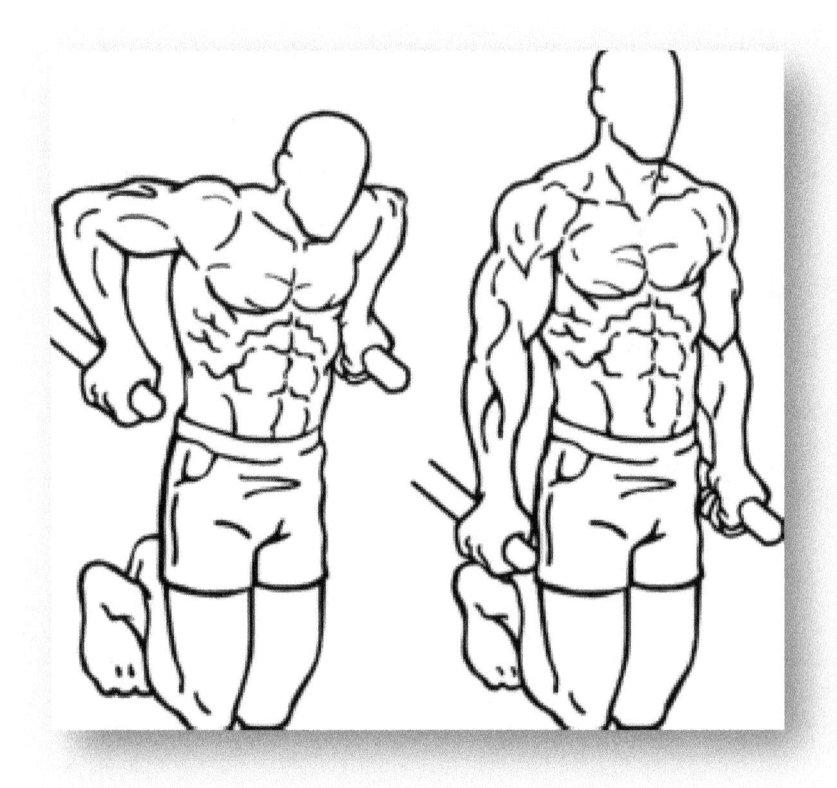

Bar dips is the most favorite exercise among all fitness lovers and professional athletes. This body weight exercise is an essential part of calisthenics and gymnastics that mainly targets upper body muscles.

Instructions:

* Stand in between parallel bars and grasp the bars with your both hands
* Lift your whole body off the ground by straightening your arms
* Bend your knees and cross them
* Now, lower your body by bending your arms at a distance from where you can easily move up to starting position to complete one rep
* Do 12 to 15 reps in each set
* Complete 3 to 4 sets

"L" Hold Bar Dips

"L" hold bar dips being an advance technique of bar dips that not only targets upper body muscles, but also target abdominal core muscles.

Instructions:

* Hold a bar dips position while lifting your body off the ground
* Raise your legs to make a 90 degree angle between your raised legs and abdomen
* Now, lower and raise your body by bending and straightening your arms respectively to complete one rep
* Do at least 12 to 15 reps
* Repeat this exercise 3 to 4 times

High Bar Swings

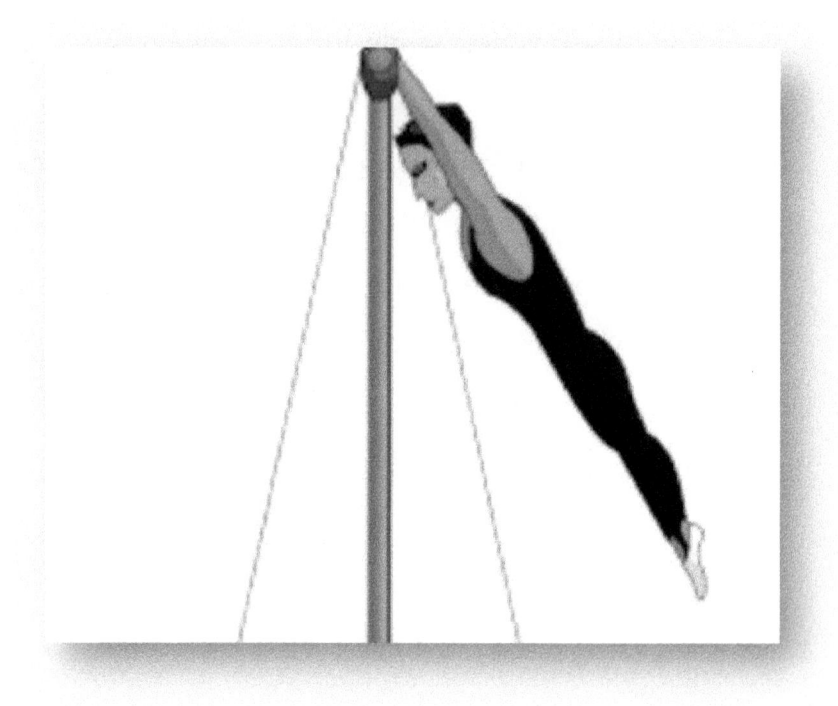

In gymnastics and calisthenics, upper body including core strength and stability is the key to progress. High bar swings strengthen upper body muscles.

Instruction:

* Hold a high bar with your hands shoulder-width apart
* Keep your both legs straight and close to each other
* Tie a rope around your wrist and the bar to avoid falling while swinging on the bar
* Now, jerk slightly to move your whole body back and forth like a swing
* Control your movement with the help of your hands
* Do not bend your arms while swinging to avoid any injury
* Swing with your legs for a better swing like an athlete

Inverted "L" hold Toe Touching

Inverted "L" hold toe touching is a core strengthening exercise that targets abdominal core muscles.

Instructions:

* Start by lying on your back
* Raise your both legs skywards in order to make a shape like "L"
* Now, lift your upper body in upward direction to touch your toes with your hands while keeping your legs straight and then quickly move back to starting position
* Complete a set with maximum reps
* Complete 3 sets

Frog Jumping

A body weight exercise that primarily targets lower body muscles especially thighs.

Instructions:

* Start by sitting on your feet with your hands on your back
* Hold your one hand with other
* Now, moderately start jumping and moving forward
* Do not stand completely while jumping (try to keep your jump not more than one foot high)
* Jump 10 to 15 steps forward in each set or according to your fitness level
* Complete 3 sets

Crocodile Raise

A great core exercise that not only burns extra abdominal fat, but also strengthens core muscles and shape them as well.

Instructions:

* Lie on your belly with your hands near your hips and your hand palms flat on the ground while facing your fingers towards your upper body
* Join your both feet together and raise your upper body without moving your lower body from pelvis by straightening your arms (like a crocodile)
* Hold this position for 10 to 15 seconds each time
* Repeat three times

Bench Crocodile Raise

Bench crocodile raise is an advance form of crocodile raise. This fascinating exercise is performed on a bench to exert extra stress on back muscles.

Instructions:

* Lie on a bench on your belly with your lower body on the bench and your upper body in the air
* Use something to anchor your feet to support your crocodile raise (you can ask your friend to hold your feet firmly to support you)
* Rest your both hands on your back
* Raise your upper body in the same way in standard crocodile raise
* Hold this position for 2 seconds and then move back to starting position to complete one rep
* Do 8 to 10 reps
* Repeat this exercise not more than two times to avoid back pain and neck strain
* You can use hyperextension bench or a simple sitting bench (simple sitting bench is more challenging than hyperextension bench)

Modified Zu-bu Stance

Zu-bu is a popular stance of WUSHU martial arts. It is also known as empty stance because in this stance we exert all our weight on our rear leg and put no weight on front leg.

Instructions:

* Stand straight with your one foot ahead and the other foot back
* Bent your rear leg and point your knee outward about 45° while keeping your front knee straight or slightly bent (front straighten leg exerts extra stress on your rear leg muscles)
* This stance is slightly different from Zu-bu stance where you have to bend both your legs. In this stance, you just need to straighten your front leg to exert extra stress on the back leg
* Hold this position for 2 to 3 seconds and move back to standing position, and then again hold Zu-bu stance to complete one rep
* Do the same for the other leg
* Do 10 to 15 reps for each leg

Side Leg Raise

Side leg raise is an effective flexibility and calisthenics exercise that targets gluteus medius, gluteus minimus, and tensor fasciae latae.

Instructions:

* Start by standing near a pole or a chair for support
* Rest your feet at little wider than your shoulder width
* Now, moderately raise your one leg sidewise as high as you can with ease while keeping the other leg straight, and then move back to starting position to complete one rep
* Do 12 to 15 reps for each leg

Back Leg Raise

Back leg raise targets lower back muscles including hips, thighs, and abdominal muscles.

Instructions:

* Stand straight with your face towards the wall or the pole you are going to use as a support
* Rest your both hands to the wall or grip the pole firmly while keeping your chest towards the pole
* Step your one leg slightly forward as compared to the other
* Now, kick back in a moderate manner as high as you can easily while keeping your head up and shoulders stretch outwards
* try your best to move your kick back slowly than you kick up
* do 12 to 15 reps each time for both legs
* repeat this exercise 3 times or more if you have extra or unpleasant fat on your hips

Front Leg Raise

Front leg raise is a body weight or calisthenics exercise that targets your lower body muscles especially front thigh muscles and abdominal core muscles.

Instructions:

* Stand straight by resting your upper and lower back with the pole or, a wall or something else
* Try to tack your whole body on the pole including your back and legs
* Hold the pole with both your hands over your head to support your movement
* Now, raise your one leg as high as you can without moving and bending the other leg
* Do 10 to 15 reps for each leg
* Repeat this exercise 3 times for each leg

Dragon Flag

Dragon flag is an advance core exercise that is also known as hardest core and body weight exercise.

Instructions:

* Lei down on your back on a bench with something fixed to grip firmly (over your head)
* Grip the fix position with your hands little wider than your shoulder width for better balance and drive your both legs up straight (without bending your knees)
* Raise your legs as high as possible and try to raise all your body up with your legs except your upper back and then move back to starting position
* Do as many reps as you can
* Repeat this exercise 3 times or less
* Do not bend your waist to correctly perform this exercise

Chapter 5

Supplementation for Overall Health and Fitness

---

you are serious about transforming your body, you really need to train and eat in a proper way to develop new lean muscle mass while getting rid of unwanted fat. But training hard can diminish your body of minerals, vitamins, and other substances necessary for muscle gain and fat burning. In spite of the best diet possible, it is usually extremely hard to have all these essential elements, and that is where supplements come in.

Therefore, here are the best supplements that are worth your money.

Fish Oil

Fish oil is proven to improve the immune system and brain performance, protect against muscle breakdown, boost joint recovery, and even promote fat burning. The human body can produce several vitamins, nutrients naturally, fish oil is a thing we are not able to make naturally, and, therefore, you really need to supplement to deliver your body with what you need.

Vitamin D

If you do not go out in direct sunlight enough (preferably for at least 20 minutes daily between the hours of 10 am to 2 pm when the sun's rays are most effective) you are likely to end up with vitamin D deficiency. This raises your possibilities of obesity, stimulates a decrease in muscle mass and makes you more sensitive to lots of health conditions. In accordance with a research, men with sufficient vitamin D have better testosterone levels, the leanest body composition, a higher percentage of lean mass and better overall wellness compared to those with inadequate vitamin D.

Whey Protein

You can get a good amount of protein in your diet, but protein powder has other benefits: It's handy and usually lower in calories than a whole high protein meal. Whey protein does undoubtedly provide some other distinctive advantages; it's full of the ever crucial branched chain amino acids (BCAA's), which can play a vital role in muscle development, muscle recovery, and you've got an ideal, on the go meal that takes a minute to prepare.

Probiotics

All of us eat a lot of food daily; however, we really pay attention to our digestion. Healthy gut bacteria play a vital role in general health, digestive system, and immunity process. Specifically, probiotics can help rejuvenate and nurture our internal supply of beneficial bacteria. Moreover, this will result in less gas, stomach pain, and irritation. There are actually incredible numbers of different ranges of bacteria in our guts. Probiotics help in keeping a healthy GI ecosystem and keep everything in balance.

Creatine

This artificial type of an energy source generated naturally in the body is stored in the muscles to be used during exercise. Moreover, it is proven to work! Several studies demonstrate that creatine does help speed restoration and the development of lean muscle mass after an exercise session. Creatine also brings more water into your muscle cells, adding a stretch on the cell that will increase long-lasting growth. Lately, creatine is identified to raise levels of insulin, like growth factor in muscles, which is important for revitalizing growth.

Green Tea

One thing that many people don't really know is that green tea fights fat. Scientific studies have demonstrated that animals who are given extract get less weight and shed more fat than animals who are given a placebo, and if it is suitable for the animals it's suitable for us as well. Experts preferably recommend almost eight glasses daily which is hard to follow for many people, so go for the simplest way and only take a supplement.

Multivitamins

They might not be the most essential supplements out there, but they're still among the most vital, particularly for all those that don't eat sufficient vegetables and fruits. Try to choose multi-vitamin supplements that are directed precisely, without the extra iron since extra amounts of this mineral cause heart disease. You can normally find just one tablet that has 100% of your daily requirement, supplying as many vitamins and minerals as possible.

Magnesium

Having sufficient amounts of magnesium helps in maximum overall performance since the body is better able to use energy and carry out muscular contractions. Study shows supplementing with magnesium boosts red blood cell production, makes zinc more accessible to aid in energy production and muscle contractions, and encourages the elimination of waste products produced by intense exercise, making it possible for you to recover faster.

Zinc

Zinc is essential because it is a mineral present in every tissue in your body. It's a highly effective antioxidant, encouraging to protect against cancer, and is usually directly associated with the upkeep of hormone levels, which is necessary for muscle development and fat loss. Zinc plays an important role in protein synthesis, and sufficient amounts enable a more powerful release of the three most essential anabolic hormones: growth hormone, testosterone, and insulin. Without having sufficient amounts of these hormones, you'll miss out on muscle and strength development of your hard work in the gym.

Finish

Thank you again for downloading this book!

I hope this book was able to help you improve your health and physique.

The next step is to apply what you learned and take massive amount of action.

Finally, if you enjoyed this book, then I'd like to ask you for a favor, would you be kind enough to leave a review for this book on Amazon? It'd be greatly appreciated!

Thank you and good luck!

CLICK HERE TO LEAVE A REVIEW
http://amzn.to/1Ymioj1

View more books from **ARNOLD YATES**

Bodybuilding: How to Easily Build Muscles and Keep Mass Permanently: 10X your Results and Build the Physique That You Want.

CLICK HERE
to give me your image and get the 10% discount
http://bit.ly/1VChksV
https://knowledgeforgreatness.leadpages.co/gb/